OBSCENELY

YOURS

OBSCENELY YOURS

ANGELO NIKOLOPOULOS

Alice James Books
FARMINGTON, MAINE
www.alicejamesbooks.org

10 9 8 7 6 5 4 3 2 1

Alice James Books are published by Alice James Poetry Cooperative,
Inc., an affiliate of the University of Maine at Farmington.

Alice James Books
238 Main Street
Farmington, ME 04938
www.alicejamesbooks.org

Library of Congress Cataloging-in-Publication Data
Nikolopoulos, Angelo.
  Obscenely Yours / Angelo Nikolopoulos.
    pages cm
  ISBN 978-1-882295-99-9 (pbk. : alk. paper)
  I. Title.
  PS3614.I557O27 2013
  811'.6--dc23
                                        2012043072

Alice James Books gratefully acknowledges support from
individual donors, private foundations, the University of Maine at
Farmington, and the National Endowment for the Arts.

ART WORKS.
arts.gov

Cover Image: Wayne Koestenbaum, *Angel with Blue Wings*, 2011,
acrylic and newspaper on canvas. Courtesy of the artist.

TABLE OF CONTENTS

A Lover This Coarse

The Garden of Sweden

ACKNOWLEDGMENTS

Grateful acknowledgment is made to the editors of the following journals and anthologies in which these poems, often in different forms, originally appeared:

The Awl: "Hot Interracial, Hard Fuck, Big Black Cook"
The Best American Poetry 2012: "Daffodil"
Best New Poets 2011: "Daffodil"
Boston Review: "Self Suck"
Boxcar Poetry Review: "Forced Entry: Auditions"
   (published as "Whispering Pines, Texas")
Collective Brightness: "A Divine Spirit That Indwells in Nature
   and the Universe" and "Fisting: Treading the Walls"
The Cortland Review: "After the Burial"
Fence: "Obscenely Yours: Scene One, Scenes Two and Three,
   Scene Four, Scene Five, Scenes Six and Seven, Scene Eight,
   Deleted Scene"
The Gay & Lesbian Review: "Rear Stable: Auditions"
   (published as "Asshole")
The Journal: "Still, my desire has made me. . ."
The Los Angeles Review: "www.daddyhunt.com"
Meridian: "Letter"
Mudfish: "Take the Body Out"
The New York Quarterly: "Anonymous Creampies: Auditions"
   (published as "Paros, 1997")
North American Review: "Washington Square Park"

I am indebted to Alex Dimitrov, Wayne Koestenbaum, Deborah
Landau, Monica McClure, Meghan O'Rourke, Sharon Olds,
Ekoko Omadeke, D.A. Powell, and Brenda Shaughnessy for their
guidance and support; to the board and staff of Alice James Books
and to the Saltonstall Arts Colony, where many of these poems
began; and to my friends and families, both inherited and chosen,
for their humor, warmth, and gorgeous brazenness.

OBSCENELY YOURS

TAKE THE BODY OUT

for Sharon

But I love the body.
Even before the arm and leg buds appeared

in the fifth week after they made me
inside the mouth's outline

my tongue's rough draft
where I'd first learn pleasure and need

through the lips in sequence—
liquids before solids, milk before steel tip

and split pea soup, cotton-edged quilt
to stubbled frame of mouth.

I love the body
bookended by introduction and conclusion

where we learned in high school
to imbed our details:

in his beech-blond desk bored with Pythagoras
he'd lean forward

and I'd love the body that wasn't mine:
raised spine rack

his blemished neck.
And in the pine bunk of a summer's retreat

he'd tear the Velcro strip of his trunks
to reveal saltwater skin

goosefleshed thighs.
I loved his body even in its absence

in the flattened sheets
the red-scratched thread marks between fingers

in the sweaty folds behind both knees—
the mites' burrowing.

                         My own body
laid bare and harboring

as in the moments after it was born
flecked with impurities—

part glassmith, part sand-molten form.
Spread the ointment

generously over the body.
Burn your sheets, the nurse ordered.

But how could I
after our bodies had met in the sedge

and reeds of adolescence
on memory's moss-grown knotted mattress

where the imprints of our mouths still lie
wet and pressed—

how could I burn them now?

DIRECTOR'S CUT

But Love has pitched his mansion in
The place of excrement

—WILLIAM BUTLER YEATS

II

The first thing we love is a scene—

        a well-lit place where ravishing happened.

The Sabine women.

The Lovers' dogpile.

        A crude analogy?

        Love's an embarrassment then.

Both flummox and coxcomb—

taxonomically: Celosia.

        The bloom of outbreak, flaring up.

What fascinates is a body *in situation*.

A bright-colored fetish. A mar.

        The soul's rosacea spot.

OBSCENELY YOURS

SCENE ONE

It's not forced entry if you're dressed up,
fantasy's fledgling

in your ski-masked kitsch—
lose the props. More interiority

and less Times Square.
Think stranded by the river.

Think busted flat, house in the woods.
Better yet, think less.

Even premeditation's a kind of script.
Come in and use my phone?

I want it to startle, this offering.

ANONYMOUS CREAMPIES: AUDITIONS

When windows opened it was a consolation

and those mornings my windows opened

to bougainvillea vines against white walls

that I would trace with my small hands

and collect their petals, thin as paper,

to stuff into books, the folds of beds,

my mother's purse. I'd seal them into letters

that summer to send to friends in the states.

Purple lanterns from Capri, I wrote.

That summer, the found octopus

we inked against a rock. At night it hung

from wire. That summer, the man I'd find

out where the sea met the island at night

and I would not tell a soul—

how could you tell a mother, after collecting

your purple lanterns, after having hung

them up to dry against the bare white wall

where you had met him in the salty night

and you had asked him to take you quickly.

//

I've never tried bliss before.

The manifolds make it impossible.

I was wearing a black peacoat
with the collar turned up and falling down,
whistling to Tequila.

Being single,
everything withers in the bud.

Perhaps it would be nice for a man
of sufficient means to happen along,
to materialize.

You were in monochrome.

TRANS AMORE: AUDITIONS

Her summer dress was a hillside in bloom.
Pastel print of gladiolas and allium bathed

in a ginkgo leaf's green, ruffled around
the bodice, an afternoon held by its white seams

that I would try on, feet first through the sheath,
to know what it was like, a season on your body.

My mother, in her summer dress, after the dishes
were in their cupboards, after her sons had been put

to sleep, where they tussled and snagged the sheets
with their feet, she was kind. She'd let me flit

in the night, on her cobblestone girlhood streets,
through the meadow in our hem-held loitering.

The cowslips shameless across our knees.

OBSCENELY YOURS

SCENES TWO AND THREE

I like it better when I'm unconscious—
sexsomnia's ontology, hard

copula of possibility, to be.
In this dream I'm Farm Girl Walking.

Goldenrod. Milkweed.
Beyond the barn where the workmen

lunch in the open field.
Rye morsel. Tin canteen. Aren't you

the prettiest girl we ever seen?
Wet animal smell.

You need the particulars. They matter.
Daybreak enters.

My shoes, I didn't leave them there.
I left them here.

—

In another you are Man Bending
Over Echinacea Plot,

one hand collecting
what the other hand pulls out.

Yellowing bundle. Pliant stalks.
You choose so easily

what will give
from what needs leaving alone.

The root's gnarl, upward gasp of no.
From my window

I'm loosened just by watching you.
Rusted wheelbarrow.

Clump of fist.
When you reach for me, promise—

you'll reach for me like this.

BOYS DESTROYED: AUDITIONS

My world of boys revolved around spit,

the palmed bet-glue, brawl beginner—

insult's first cousin. The farthest loogie ruled

the club. So when he spit on my back once

and I heard the thrill of his larynx clearing

and releasing, like an engine left in disuse finally

revving, leaving behind a spotted trail of smoke,

I understood that sometimes when a man

fucks another man, it is something else entirely.

It is the last one on the court, the rotten egg;

it is the quickest mile, the highest jump,

the cheese stands alone; it is smear the queer,

the mouth's final drawl: *I am bigger than you,*

I am faster than you, and I will always beat you.

//

But aren't we charming when we're inconsolable
and thrashing at the stars?

> You caught my eye at French Roast.
> (Boy in Red Plaid.)

I can get so hysterical.

> If you see this, let me know.

At a café once, my waiting
turned flammable.

A soup to stir.

> A bed of straw.

> And though he was tepid,
> I was nuclear runoff.

A lead-rimmed cocktail.

> If you see this, you should know:

I became so fretful and fettered

> I swallowed
> my own food-poisoned heart.

SERVICING SENIORS: AUDITIONS

At thirteen I'd listen to my brother's friends
list the things their girlfriends did to them.

They blew, gave head and hummers, slobbed
on knobs, smoked poles, and deep-throated.

And I'd imagine it literally: the lips siphoned
and wedged like a valve, the white-hot iron

of it, moiled cautery. The throat's damming.
Out by the shed where they took them at night

I thought their mouths became something else,
extraordinary and separate, functioning apart

from the thin girl-frame, the loose halter.
They became all mouth. In time one would teach

me other terms for it. The skull-fuck. Cock
worship. The human urinal. Out by the shed

where he took me at dusk, I'd line myself up
against the row of girls, beneath the sawdust-

coppered night, where I'd look up from my place
on the floor, amazed by our brassy pliancy.

FISTING: TREADING THE WALLS

—

Strange euphemism:
the silent duck, the hand made

into beak and inched inward,
and upward,

becoming natant and buoyant,
treading the walls

of column and canal.
Though wall's not accurate at all

but how else to know the thing
if not through symbolism?

—

Why else call the ass
the lumen—

the light snared
by fold and slit, luminous

flux of musculature

and valve, a star cluster
of enclosure—

if not to become arm
deep in metaphor?

—

The side prayer:
doubly benevolent

and palm to palm,
the handler,

mighty yet gentle,
piston and pastor,

administers his hands
to the desire

of every living thing.
Open for me

my lover, my dove.

—

But analogy's not enough,
like skiff to port, flock to paddock,

the harboring ass—
to know is to touch the thing itself.

O doubting Thomas, good for you.

Refusing the good news, the false
Messiah, until he came for you.

*Reach out your hand and put it into
my side*, he said, *and believe.*

II

It's a darling thought,
annihilation—
to swoon, to immolate.

The body wettening
itself on the edge

of the abyss.

But I'm unapologetically
raptured without you.

My aloneness is tender,
the soul's hangnail.

Where there is a wound
there is a subject,

Roland says.

And I ingest so many
things in one small day.

Lettuce, smoke, white wine
from the freezer.

Ephemeral,
distilled spirit.

I'm easy membrane.

BROTHER KNOWS BEST: AUDITIONS

Sunday morning, our socks wet and balled,
the rings around our ankles red with dirt
and mother complaining of the smell in our
bedroom, offering fried eggs, but we lay
instead doing what, listened to music, tossed
a ball against the wall? It was an awful fluttering
how he'd lock the door and put himself inside
my mouth, and I'd stare at the unmade bed,
his worn boxing gloves, until he had finished.
At night I'd imagine it: the blond hairs
on his legs, the weight of his torso beating into me,
quietly at first, then quicker in his rushing—
leaping over rocks, struggling through branch
and crevice and wind, until he had reached it.
This mountain he had climbed to let out a cry
from above, as if he'd won, that he had earned it.
I watched him at his terrible height from below.

STR8 GYM BUDDIES

for Mark

You can smell them from here—
the alloyed bench press,

iron beam and barbell, the grainy grip
of blister and callous.

It's sinful synesthesia,
the hour spent in repetition and set,

extending their core—
cable raise, dead lift, upright row—

friction's copper wire
coiled and uncoiled by lateral lunge thrust,

until failure, until sore. What's voyeurism,
after all, but a lesson in resistance?

To lower your face
into that reddened strain of burden.

One more. Give me one more.
I could go on like this, too.

I love the language of cardiovascular desire,
looking's syntax in its steeliness,

tethered by limits, wrought form.
The threadbare cotton

of endurance spread over deltoids,
pivoting breastbone.

But if description's just encoded want,
why not decode the dénouement?

That muffled sigh of fatigue,
his index fingers curled to guide

the weight into its lock—
the way he slumps over, reveals the thin

crest of waist, between underwear
band and shirt,

and I rest the brim of my feeling there,
across the skin,

the tan line,
the few blond sprouting hairs.

OBSCENELY YOURS

SCENE FOUR

In any other dungeon I'd try
pirate and native, landlord and tenant,

anything but this—
master and servant's too Depeche Mode.

That's easy, the eighties' garishness.
Let's be Gorean instead,

feudalism's kink—
my tyrant, the castle's outlaw

in your sword-grown sovereignty.
I'll carry the homestone, polish the filigree.

I enjoy my womanly things.
In the glebe where I sow the land

I'll harvest your name from the wind.
I accept these parameters.

You've kept me famished for weeks.

//

I'm using the language of argumentation
because what else is there?

        Nowhere Bar and on the street.

        I enjoyed being in the restroom with you.

When someone asks you to love him,
you are being asked to be more you.

        You were blond with a beard.

        A tattoo on the back.

Sunday morning and I pour myself
a cup of misanthropy.

        I was Latino, 20 and shy.

REAR STABLE: AUDITIONS

When I saw mine for the first time

in the tilted view of a compact mirror

I felt cheated, bored almost, having expected

something cavernous, something more alive,

but finding it taut, instead, like the stretched

rubber of a racquet ball. It was its lifelessness

that bothered me, how it adhered there, as inert

as a postcard, and I wondered how could it be

this that he loved most, why he spoke of it

so affectionately. *Show me daddy's sweet asshole,*

he'd say. Perhaps he knew better, being older,

having met me in my bathing shorts that summer,

my body thin and undeveloped, the younger

of two boys. Perhaps he saw possibility—

examining my parts like the bulk of a cedar,

his hands over bark, a sticky droop of sap.

I'd rivet my torso over his enormous knee,

grip the solid stalk of his calves, and let his fingers

work into me, until I became something else:

a stained letter box, the smooth curved handle

        of a shovel. With linseed oil and pain

and delight littered in pools around our feet

        he would make a thoroughbred out of me.

A LOVER THIS COARSE

That accident which pricks me

—ROLAND BARTHES

SUB CUB HUMILIATED: AUDITIONS

The shame-boil when he saw it, as coarse

as a follicle pushing forth from its bulb,

shaving's uselessness. His stethoscope dull

on my chest's prickly growth. I turned my head

to the left and memory accomplished

its imperceptible trick, alloying the day we tried

them on in his white Chrysler, the dangling

latex unused at the tip, like turkey necks we said

and pointed. He called it boy's stuff, the skin's

dry patch, stiff aftermath of our bodies' cultivating.

I hated it for its plainness, the mirror's matter-

of-factness. My kindred, my double, who rubbed

himself over the sink, until there it was—

against the marble, inside the parked Chrysler,

in the cold examining room where I pardoned

myself beneath the light. *I never asked for this.*

//

How do you love, finally?

You in your room redolent
of unlucky things—

I'm sorry the restroom wasn't big enough.

Lucky is vulgar.

Shot in the dark here:
You and your fantastic dog—

you who search for love
make manifest your own loveliness.

Wear something red tomorrow
and I'll be sure to make a move.

That gentlemanly art.

You live in New Jersey, too.

OBSCENELY YOURS

SCENE FIVE

If two men look out the same prison bars
and one sees stars

where the other sees mud,
I'd say check your telescope at the door,

sweetcheeks, I'm into recidivism.
Your bad choices,

my clean slate make for a saucy Venn diagram.
Aren't we hypothetically?

You're more likely to die
in an elevator shaft or a baseball pickle

than inside my lynchpin,
my striped lovely, closet tickle monster.

So here's hoping for moping—
I prefer the volta to the easy-breezy give in.

Don't force it for the warden.

DAFFODIL

Don't you know, sweetheart,
less is more?

Giving yourself away
so quickly

with your eager trumpet—
April's rentboy

in your flock of clones,
unreasonably cheerful, cellulose,

as yellow as a crow's foot—*please*.
I don't get you.

Maybe it's me,
always loving what I can't have,

the bulb refusing itself,
perennial challenge.

I'd rather have mulch
than three blithe sepals from you.

I've never learned
how to handle kindness

from strangers.
It's uncomfortable, uncalled-for.

I'm into piss and vinegar,
brazen disregard,

the minimum wage indifference
of bark, prickly pear.

Flirtation's tension:
I dare, don't dare.

But what would you know
about restraint,

binge drinking
your way through spring,

botany's twink bucked
by lycorine, lethal self-esteem?

You who come and go
with the seasons,

bridge and tunnel.
You're all milk and no cow—

intimacy for beginners.
The blond-eyed boy stumbling home.

If I were you, I'd pipe down.
Believe me,

I've bloomed like you before.

FORCED ENTRY: AUDITIONS

There are men 'round these parts who would kill us,
I joked. *They'd tie us to the tail ends of their pickup*
       trucks and drag us through gravel. It happens.
Your mother would too, he said, sealing the last
       mesh panel of our tent and having had the better
joke fell heavily into sleep. A little summer
       moonlight broke through with its easy tenderness
but I lay awake, instead, imagining that a mob
       was assembling, that there were men in those hills
with unkempt eyebrows and rope and fire and spit
       on the ground, and my mother was among them—
certain that there was whispering among the pines
       as they sifted themselves against the thistle,
and she was there too, wild-eyed and unmoving,
       sensing our bodily heat, our pitiful heartbeats.
They would wait for me to sleep, I knew, before
       entering to find us, two men discovered—
where they would take him from me and into darkness,
       beyond the boathouse, and she would come for me
with torch and hitch knot and love-blackened heart.
       The mother who bends to loosen a tooth.

//

I wonder which is the more horrible.

        Beer goggles. My year of farcical thinking.
        At the No Tell Motel

I met a man
who was impossible and cross.

        He loved me.
        And then, famously, he did not.

I've spent the day in a bar of louche milieu—
a naughty practical joke.

        My heaviness is a petulant boy,
        quite the gold digger.

But I swat the dept away.
I'm not going to buy you a drink, my dear.

        Not yet, anyway.

DIORAMA, *HOMO ERECTUS HUNTING*

Bone spear. Arrow. Broken antler.
What would I know

       to do with them?
       In my unwashed natural state,

lacking fangs, claws, horns, hooves,
fire-hardened tusks—

       nature's weakling.
       I like to cry, feel sorry for myself.

And for the boar,
wooden pole through the mouth,

       brown blot fringed by goldenrod,
       aster, blazing star—

the soft, easy things never culled
into history,

       lost in the strata of our record.
       Unlike this boar,

resurrected here
in mineralized bones and teeth,

       that I'd be prepared to skin,
       if I had to.

II

Let's face it, multiplicity's silly—
romance's Rubik's cube.

> So let's get serious.
> How are your thighs?

You: auburn and curly.
Me: shaved, driver's cap, bestie in tow.

> I thought we made a connection
> after Mass. Did you?

> Sure, I'm lonely too—
> but I'm professional and frugal.

I'll take plenty of none.
I prefer minimalism, modernism's truth.

> Than to be beholden. Say it.
> Beholden sounds olden.

One's father with a cup.
I'd rather split the bark.

HOT INTERRACIAL, HARD FUCK, BIG BLACK COOK

—*XTUBE VIDEO TITLE*

And why not—
when it's a scrambling, isn't it?

Kidney shuffle, blowing one's beans,
overture of parts,

dry to wet, mouth-whisked
and body-beaten to barmy foam.

Though this cook's no regard
for precise ratios:

2 parts meat : 1 part yolk, and so forth.
It's soulful improvisation,

a dash of this, fistful of that,
a finger in every pink-teemed pot,

since math makes no good art.
Not typo then,

unforgivable swap of nouns,
but something Freudian,

a slip into the bread and butter
of relations,

simple reduction:
how we lump our parts together

willy-nilly and sweat-streaked,
a sloppy alchemy,

and hope for the best—
these profligate limbs on the mealy sheets

left to rise leavened and browned.
In the morning

we will depart wholesome again.

//

If midnight is the hour for lovers

                              illuminate me beloved
the court's yours—

wordless in your hooded orb

                              embowered thing

                my lost Matryoshka doll.

                              I like a man in Lycra
so make a move.

But you're the world's

                              worst tennis mate

                soul mate—

                              double-faulted
                refusing the net, dead net.

It's always love-all.

                              Why not sulk

in my sensory deprivation tank, loveless?

                Me and my bulky
                              perception
threshold.

What I take on faith I take lightly—

bee wing, dull pin prick,
                    scent in a ten-room home.

                        You were a voyeur
in Central Park.

            How should I know?

My senses are dull
                        flirt illiterate.

                    Better off moonless—
no itch, no impulse.

In my saline vale

                            I float.

DUDES ON CAMPUS

BERKELEY, CA

My cherry lips have often kiss'd
thy stones too, P and T—big whoop.

When the Campanile chimes its bells at noon
we bottleneck beneath Sather Gate

against elbows and flyers and our blatant youth.
It's all very tiring,

the self made public and obvious.
Who needs eucalyptus groves and Strawberry Creek?

I detest the sun's etiquette.
Let's celebrate the basement bathroom instead

where we wait in that darkened bower,
creaky ship hull, pressed against

the stall's buffered edge.
Until there it comes, through the opening,

dumb and quiet. Where it's easy to adore most
that which goes unsaid—

loving drape of silence, anonymity's pledge—
to put yourself

through a chink in a wall and have kindness
greet you on the other end.

WWW.DADDYHUNT.COM

—

Because preference implies power,
there is body type, dick length, sexual role.

You want daddy or hunter,
average or horse hung, top or bottom.

Sometimes versatile. You can search
by age range, body hair, and *looking for*:

blue collar, ex-smoker, within five miles
of [enter zip code]. You send *gropes*

to members to say *I'm interested.*
I'm looking. In the top left corner,

my yellow mailbox blinks. TopDad4U
types, *Horned verbal jock. Hosting.*

—

To host, to receive, to entertain guests.
So you travel to the Upper West Side

by wet underground, red line express,
where you are rewarded, this time,

by handsome face, height/weight proportional.
A leather harness. So you obey,

chin up to receive the host, as in wafer,
holy Eucharist, the cold marble

of childhood beneath you,
but now the language more reciprocal—

the jeans parted down to the thighs
to give, and to be given, the body.

———

On the subway ride home, it is not guilt
that hangs overhead, not regret soiled

in the folds of the shirt, the torn buttonhole.
It is wonder, instead, and lineage.

I imagine the long row of men before me
in their muslin shirts, trimmed beards,

and Nixon is president.
It is the lull and glow of the Hudson

where they'd feel through darkness,
over damp planks, until they hit body—

chest, torso, legs—and that was that.
You, I'm so happy to have found you.

—

But I'm surprised how they managed
to find each other at all

in that wet secrecy
until I am brought back to sixteen

where I stand at the foot of a ladder
and there is a man, a worker,

halfway up, the sweat moving down
the bicep, and the eyes—

not even the eyes—
beyond the limen, a soul on all fours:

Whatever you want, I'll give you.
Whatever you want, it's yours.

OBSCENELY YOURS

SCENES SIX AND SEVEN

I can't stop thinking about your safeword.

It's too red.

    Rhubarb.

    Shallot skin.

    Rufous Twistwing.

Isn't discipline about subtlety?

We've hedged our edges so let's play on them.

Remember that the next time we're switching.

Even red-faced in subspace—

    I won't say it.

        —

    But what's glove got to do with it?

    Neoprene's hand dam, latex primness.

    Isn't pig play abstract expressionism?

    Eager bottom, messy canvas.

    Or is all play artifice, linguistic form?

    Subject   Verb   Object

    Debbie does Dallas. Daddy likes Gravy.

    I like it when you talk structuralism.

    Your big fat red mouth, dirty speech act.

SELF SUCK

Maybe more's not merrier but messier,
since you can be your own

object and taste of desire, both surrender
and control in one wet exchange.

Intimacy's frontbend: the torso strong-
armed against wall or swivel chair

until the sex dips into the same body's
mouth. It's like watering

and being watered at the same time.
Fall seven times

and you'll stand up full. Slippery logic:
the snake who ate its tail.

Maybe it's the true preservationism,
cutting out the middleman—

him or her—making it local and organic,
pleasure's Trader Joe's.

But sustainability's never sexy,
canvas clad in its carbon-cock-blocking.

If you can't save the penguins please yourself,
objectivism's golden rule.

To be volition and validation, lover and lovee,
a recipient handing himself money.

But a party of one's no fun—
even autoeroticism's depressing.

Like a return to the wellspring of childhood,
where we confronted it face-first,

our awful cub scout truth,
that we enter the valley unchartered and alone

and we must leave it this way, too.

II

Won't you dance with me then

on the corner of squalor

                    and poverty?

        I am thinking of my father

poor and dying.

Isn't this a feeling

                    made for two?

                What are you into?

                    You are

    taken

            but open

1300 feet away

                            discreet

I am visiting

                        new to town

        looking

for friends   activity partners

THE GARDEN OF SWEDEN

Father!

—TOM OF FINLAND

TRUE BEAUTY'S EASY TO FORGET

When it's yourself who's looking
and looked at—

a myopic knowing in the morning,
sleep struck and shocked—

this is my face!
Unshareable, one-of-a-kind blandness.

Alone in my apartment
I'm the prettiest boy in the room.

So why should you be one, too?
Better-face made better

by the arrangement of unequal things.
A strange beauty so foreign

it makes my heart sting. Jealousy,
a kind of locked-in syndrome.

But in the waiting room where I lurk
for Lasik of the soul,

I believe it's a miracle to have been
given a body at all.

Life is a celebration. By neon lights
and cellulite. We are not dead.

//

           Still, my desire has made me
radiantly unspecial—

                a spoon among spoons.

                When I am horny I go
out at night

       to the eucalyptus grove alone to stew.

That's dramatic but it's local.

                  If it's my darkness
that matters,

                  I'll matter the dark too,
the way plants do.

        I like the soggy moss,

             the diaphanous foghorn.

             It makes me feel naked

        and molecular. Look,

here's what it's come to:

                you are safe and dry
somewhere else,

       and I'm tired of being a ten-fingered

thing, belligerent.

I am waiting and I am feminized

—a simple darling—

I'd fill our house

with innumerable goods.

My washing machine.

Your box of tools.

WASHINGTON SQUARE PARK

—

Fifth Avenue, late October,
and the black-eyed Susans—
        sultry sun worshipers
mouthed by leopard slugs
        this morning—are getting
ready to break my heart.
        I don't mean to humanize,
but this perennial's collapse
        is contagious, the square's
full of it: beetled wrecking ball,
        rift and rasp of jackhammer,
sodden elm leaf, wingless spore.
        Even deeper, I imagine
the disrepair beneath the grass,
        near Hangman's Elm
in potter's field, where the Dutch
        sublet the land to freed slaves,
buried indigent and unknown
        and yellow-fevered bodies

into Minetta's tobaccoed muck—

        twenty thousand relics

rivering together in the mud-slung

        detritus, swab of root,

carbon, unhinged elbow, and ligament.

      —

Giuseppe—

           of all invasive species

you are most obvious

           being both statue and

Italian. Emancipator,

           there is always a love

story that's thwarted.

           Bronze cast and cool-

ed, the child unborn,

           Anita—both dead in

San Marino, removed.

           Wife, core pin, sprue.

The finished hollow

           —what's left of you.

—

Grief is local

                    and I walk through it inured.

                 There's the day's
cabbage-white noise: honeycombed

              layered cinder,
              trowel and bull float, a warbler's call—

one vast proof
of the obvious: things grow.

        It's undeserved

                 to have a stranger affirm my belief

                in beauty—
so I'll take it, halfheart: with aramid

            and sandblast,
            the broom and seed of prevention,

bloom and blemish.

               His body warm in its wholeness.

—

It is good that we are warm
                 and together,

but say my love to me.

The body is never enough,
                 for we can do one better,

even if it cheapens us—

before we enter the garden,
                 half-dressed and barefoot,

prepared to replace

anything,
                 the fisted hook of ivy—

say my love to me:

here in the rotted oak,
                 in the pebbled road;

inside this stem and bloom,

my darling, you will find me
                 here beneath this rock.

But I'm logistically opposed to love.

   All day the homunculus
   of desire pulses.

   My stranger.
   My shared-interest.

      If I'm a candidate, then so are you.

From its hood
our happenstance moans and moves.

      I'm tired of being my own Saint
      Sebastian of missed connections.

   Garden of Eden tonight,
   deli counter. Blue sweatpants.

A picnic to ourselves—
that's the idea, isn't it?

   (See *Women in Love*).

      Frantic and beautiful.
      The Lovers drowning in the lake.

IF NOT WITHIN, SOUL

Then out with you!
Along the edge where the skiffs park

and neighbor Pat walks his dog.
Out by the bluff

and chimney stalks of meadow rue—
to have a biopsy of it,

the day's midsection, benign happenings.
Perhaps I've been looking

for soul in all the wrong places?
In all the bodies that I have loved.

But what's there to love about you?
Will-o'-the-wisp, phosphine faerie—

the bog's strobe light.
When night falls, you're so clever

when you're ephemeral.
I'd rather have the marsh itself.

Water lovely and temperate,
as dull as a plate.

What I have loved I've loved by dimension,
by texture and sentiment.

The mouth's simple requirements.
Why want more?

At day's end, a thirst so muscular,
I'm aroused and proud—

exchanging you, again and again,
for each taut pleasure.

BREEDER FEVER: AUDITIONS

It was different in high school. We'd make
the best of ten minutes and puberty
      with our histamines, swapping saliva until
the tongue became instrument: The Slap
      Machine. The Hurricane. The Froth Maker.
His mouth made me sick and I did nothing
      but savor each symptom: the fever chills,
reddened nose blush, the smooth Amoxicillin
      down the throat like a pink ribbon. Until
the virus spread—first to mother, then father,
      then to brother—love's house of strange
invalids, each in our delicate misery.
      Because to touch each other might break us,
we'd breathe the same air and hold it in our
      chambered lungs, as if feeling were contagious.
I almost admired it. I almost wrote despised.

OBSCENELY YOURS

SCENE EIGHT

If it really is best when we regress,
why stop at infancy?

Gerber-faced lazy,
bottom heavy and safety-pinned shut—

do nothing by halves. Let's go cellular,
in our million and one

recombinations, our roving haploids.
DNA's infinite walk of shame.

If meiosis is nature's first wife-swapping,
I'll meet you at the end

of this genetic chain.
Even better, you be string and I'll be atom,

in the reactors where we're smashed
into smithereens.

Mute hydrogen. Waft of primordial sheen.
Isn't this lovely,

our centers undone, holding nothing?

//

Doesn't love insert itself with its meaty stub

in any place and every climate—

    on a pool table

    in Miami

    in desperation

    on a school night—

it's not a poetic question

    but a matter of placement

stodgy materialism

    when the beta waves

of my soul combust

    where is my adoration

my feeling—

    on the school bench

    where I gave my sex away—

    was it there?

A DIVINE SPIRIT THAT INDWELLS IN NATURE
AND THE UNIVERSE

Where else would it be? Even father's catheter

shoehorned into his bladder and the collection bag

I carry, lukewarm and snuff-colored,

with both hands to the basin. A pamphlet lists

the things I'll need—soap, water, bedside drainage bag—

to tug at the tube hanging from his loose flesh,

the blind-tipped rift from which I once came from,

microscopic and unthinking. To *indwell*,

not in compassion or spirit, but something

more helpless: how he harbored me there,

between prostate and bladder, inside himself,

and how he lets me now, unmoved as always,

return to my own beginning—as close as I'll ever get—

in the same silence where matter animates itself,

in the cold corridor of dark clouds, where stars

are born in fire and ice, and even grander still

where I hold the warm, unfeeling flesh of our lives—

I have been given this one small thing.

AFTER THE BURIAL

If sympathy is to share in the disaster,

then why delphinium

and amaranthus, bells of Ireland—

these delicate, green fists?

Why not rebar,

shreds of drywall and plywood—

why not brick?

Why not soot and slab,

to gut, to hammer out,

the corrugated steel of grief?

To gather you a parcel of wires,

rusted screws,

with difficulty, with troubled face—

the iron and stain,

this reddened tincture of oxide.

//

I'm tempted to quit but isn't art performative?

Desperation made elliptical

and flat-screen.

What brings you on today?

One must not repeat.

One must find new ways.

This conflation of boredom and hunger.

I always think I am going to be loved.

My golden light.

The dusk-maddened cows.

Failing that, an amusing man.

How can they all be yours?

You haven't swallowed them.

LETTER

for

I've been at it all day—
     belle amour, hedge fire,
great maiden's blush—

        elbow deep in rose hips,
     with damask and rambling,
        even the waxy cuticle

and hypanthium corm
     the thrush and waxwing
peck away at. All day,

        with Botanica's Roses—
     Pam's pink, salmon spray—
        and the botanists'

embedded quips:
     Dick's delight, Ida Belle
and *proud Mary, ole!*

        Oh *lady, lady gay.*
     This is how I've spent
        my day: *bowled over,*

by appointment,
     celestial and *complicata,*
especially for you—

my *purple head of rivers.*
And in *a night in June,*
fragrant with signals,

when I cannot grasp
or see you, what could I
possibly name you—

Hi neighbor, pink-a-boo?
All day from this fog-
decked desk I write

to you *Quaker star,*
my little *bean rock,*
in absence and feeling,

on *Irwin Lane*
and *twilight*—
in *prosperine's* folds.

The Dutch Provence
of my afternoon.
Remember me. Respond.

Yours—

white pearl in red

dragon's mouth.

OBSCENELY YOURS

DELETED SCENE

Look what you did.
You laughed and ruined the mood.

How's that for verisimilitude?
Our nakedness and clownface.

Shame and guilt
have their place in this world—

I've seen them burdening,
the night-veil drawn back.

And who the hell
are you to rid me of my load?

The bed is wide and water-black.
Lay them here like bone.

YOURS

in the sedge and reeds
by Nowhere Bar and in the street
by fold and slit, luminous
by pitiful heartbeat

beyond the barn
in the salty night
by mouth's final drawl
by violence

by the river
between the stars and the mud
out by the shed
in darling thought

on the mealy sheets
against the stall's buffered edge
by wrecking ball
by bright-colored fetish

at the No Tell Motel
where stars are born in fire and ice
flecked with impurities
with pain and delight

by torch and hitch knot
by love-blackened heart
in neon lights and cellulite
by shot in the dark

in the cold examining room
with iron and stain
inside this stem and bloom, my darling
by well-lit ravishing

beyond the night-veil
near dusk-maddened cows
in the valley, unchartered
by big fat red mouth

inside the parked Chrysler
fringed by goldenrod
by rope and fire and spit on the ground
by reddened tincture of oxide

on Irwin Lane and twilight
with my womanly things
by texture and by sentiment
on the corner of squalor and poverty

beyond the limen
in the fifth week after they made me
beyond the boathouse and into darkness
at day's end, holding nothing

NOTES

"//": Several of the poems in this untitled series borrow language from the film *Women in Love*, a novel by D.H. Lawrence adapted for the screen by Larry Kramer in 1969.

"Str8 Gym Buddies": The poem responds to Mark Doty's poem "Description" from *Atlantis*, published by HarperCollins Publishers, Inc., 1995.

"True Beauty's Easy to Forget": The poem mentions John Ruskin's maxim "Composition is the arrangement of unequal things."

"Washington Square Park": The poem borrows language from Mary Oliver's poem "Peonies" and from the film *Women in Love*. Guiseppe refers to the park's monument to Guiseppe Garibaldi, a 19th century Italian general who crusaded for the formation of a unified Italy. In 1970, the monument was moved 15 feet, unearthing a glass vessel containing newspaper accounts of his death.

"Breeder Fever: Auditions": The final line is from Alice Fulton's poem "About Face" from *Sensual Math*, published by W.W. Norton & Company, Inc., 1995.

"Letter": The italicized words and phrases are common names of roses.

RECENT TITLES FROM ALICE JAMES BOOKS

Mezzanines, Matthew Olzmann
Lit from Inside: 40 Years of Poetry from Alice James Books,
    Edited by Anne Marie Macari and Carey Salerno
Black Crow Dress, Roxane Beth Johnson
Dark Elderberry Branch: Poems of Marina Tsvetaeva, A Reading
    by Ilya Kaminsky and Jean Valentine
Tantivy, Donald Revell
Murder Ballad, Jane Springer
Sudden Dog, Matthew Pennock
Western Practice, Stephen Motika
me and Nina, Monica A. Hand
Hagar Before the Occupation | Hagar After the Occupation,
    Amal al-Jubouri
Pier, Janine Oshiro
Heart First into the Forest, Stacy Gnall
This Strange Land, Shara McCallum
lie down too, Lesle Lewis
Panic, Laura McCullough
Milk Dress, Nicole Cooley
Parable of Hide and Seek, Chad Sweeney
Shahid Reads His Own Palm, Reginald Dwayne Betts
How to Catch a Falling Knife, Daniel Johnson
Phantom Noise, Brian Turner
Father Dirt, Mihaela Moscaliuc
Pageant, Joanna Fuhrman
The Bitter Withy, Donald Revell
Winter Tenor, Kevin Goodan
Slamming Open the Door, Kathleen Sheeder Bonanno
Rough Cradle, Betsy Sholl
Shelter, Carey Salerno

Alice James Books has been publishing poetry since 1973 and remains one of the few presses in the country that is run collectively. The cooperative selects manuscripts for publication primarily through regional and national annual competitions. Authors who win a Kinereth Gensler Award become active members of the cooperative board and participate in the editorial decisions of the press. The press, which historically has placed an emphasis on publishing women poets, was named for Alice James, sister of William and Henry, whose fine journal and gift for writing went unrecognized during her lifetime.

DESIGNED BY MARY AUSTIN SPEAKER

Printed by Thompson-Shore
on 30% postconsumer recycled paper
processed chlorine-free